LAID BARE

P.D. LORDE

DEDICATION

I dedicate this book to my beloved mother, who taught me how to be a woman and wife, even though I resisted the lessons when they have been taught, I have utilized them daily in marriage, now that you have passed away you teach me daily that angels really do fly.

Also To my Daddy, my rock, best friend and confidant. Always. When you are no longer here to give me your wise counsel, I shall find the most prominent tree to talk to, as you will hear me through the rustling of the leaves. Mine lips to your ears only. For Eternity!

CONTENTS

P.D. LORDE

ACKNOWLEDGMENTS

To be in this moment writing these acknowledgements is extremely humbling. This book has been a long time coming and I sit here in the gratitude that its brings. Acknowledging that God, the universe and all of my supporters in this life and the next has made this book possible. I acknowledge my whole family, for their lessons, love, and wisdom. My adorable husband Richard, my sons Aaron, Richard Junior and Joshua. My Swan Sisters. Your faith in me in all of my projects has always been unyielding and impenetrable. I love you and thank you all. Adonica Simmons, Victoria Reynold Jones, and Beverly Allen. My chosen sisters for life. To my darling sister friend and true sibling Miss Karene Stewart, without you I am nothing. Its Time!

Acceleration

My youth has accelerated past me.

Every waking moment I was having fun, I was egotistical, self-interested and indulgent, I looked out for number one.

I am middle aged, A wife and mother, with a serious job. I am grateful for my adventures, but my indulgent days are gone.

I have decided that my forties
Shall be as exciting as my
twenties. Not the same, but
different, More mature, but not
sedate.

I am cultivated, mellowed, and
seasonal. I am not dead, it's not too
late.

So many of us all fall into familiarity,
Which definitely has its place, But adventure can happen at any age, my life need not be stagnant, Nor my spirit displaced.

My point. My youth has accelerated past me.
I do not want to look back.

I will do what is required to keep it moving at
home. But my "inner me" will get my
excitement back.

As good as it gets!

Love is a two way street.

It's where two people and their hearts meet.
To be involved and entwine. Both determined
to discover whether this love in genuine.

My heart was full of love for his soul,
His heart was not the body part in
control.

Love is a two way street. My dilemma, was
that only I had feet, both in, knees deep.
Wading through this loveless murky peat.

My heart was heavy, my emotions ran high.
His love on receipt felt so dry! At first it felt
good, as I was on a high. To be with you
pushed aside my lonely cries.

Now I know that your love was
cold. You seem withdrawn. This
love feels quite old. It's stale and
dry, and not purposeful in intent.

Love is a two way street, yet you
belittle my attempts to make our
love complete.

You said, this is it, you're lucky, I'm a catch
can't you see. There are plenty of women who
would kill for a man like me! I'm professional.
I have credit. I have no kids. Look at me, this
is as good as it gets, so enjoy the ride and stop
being a kid.

Love is a two way street. I have learnt now,
with someone else that's its humble, gracious
and often sweet. There is too-ing and fro-ing
and lots of compromise too.

There is listening, not bullying and blackmail
will just not do. I have empowerment, unity
and a whole heap of passion. We have love for
love sakes, and not just for fashion.

Love is a two way street.
I want to thank you, for not jumping in with
both feet. It wasn't you! You were not worthy,
In fact, you were like poisonous scurvy.

Look at me now "moved on and happy." I
rarely think of you much, but I know that
Life for you is fairly crappy.

Love is a two way street.

Thank you for educating me, on the type of
man I wanted to meet. Take heed of your
ways and be open to love.

Remember a good woman will not settle at all
in the name of love.

Beloved Swine

This man of mine, is my beloved swine, of a
husband to whom I am stuck with?

He philanders and lies, and when caught he
cries, and preaches everlasting devotion.

He kicks and swears, Blames me, as he dares
to say that I am the reason,

"It's you", he says, "for making me feel this
bad, it's because of you I seek this attention."
Its rubbish I know, I am too tired to go, so for
now I gave him a promotion.

If next time comes, his neck will be wrung
and I will pop it like a chicken. He will be
flapping for the rest of his days. And my
fabulous self will just carry on living.

Black Liberarchie

His flash brown suit flared from the knee,
His violet shirt had pretty ruffles to the cuffs,
He was My Black Liberarchie

His afro shone from sheen; My Mister was
smooth and pristine, well-groomed all the
way to his goatee.

But on the concrete floor, lay his bookie slips
torn. His shame he could not control.

The pain overflowed. This chancers lies would
be exposed. Fears realised, eyes wide, his
nose-dived.

He knew he was to blame. His gambling
addiction was his shame, now his short walk
home seemed exceedingly long,

His wife would be waiting, His Saturday soup
in the pot, she would know instantly whether
he had a good day or not.

A lot she has endured with this chancer of
hers, The gambling, the whores, black eyes
and crossed words.

His shame resurfaced, more tears
reappeared. My Black Liberarchie in his
snazzy brown suit, Seemed less snazzy and
cool, but more cold and aloof.

The hanky came out and never left his eyes.
And, I watched him drag himself home
without any pride.

Blue

Blue waves lapping, then folding and
crashing by the rocks. It reminds me of me.

I see it, relax and breathe easy.

When I smell the sea air, I remember that I
am free.

Cry

Cry,

Don't muffle your cries.

Nor try and put flood defenses for the
hurricane that runs from your eyes.

Cry,

And feel the grief from within,

Deal with your
loss, Or the
demons will set
in.

Cry,

For tears are really healing,

It shows that the life you have lost truly had
some meaning.

Cry,

And acknowledge the gift of life,

The memories that you share,

The happy times and sometimes the strife.

Cry,

As all is not lost,

The body will turn to dust,

And the spirit and your memories still lives on.

Heal,

As you will both meet again,

Grief is not an excuse to stop living,
But a reminder there is an end.

Decades of Alliance

Decades of alliance I had with you. We have
shared moments, some pain and have lived
our lives to the full.

When I was weakened by my broken heart,
you was happy to hear me out. When I was
powerless to limited finances, As a friend you
sought me out.

 As my situation improved I took you with me,
As I became less fragile and bruised, you
turned away from me.

When I finally met my true love, You became
estranged from me, Now that I am happily
married, it is your choice to disunite from me.

Decades of Alliance I have had with you.
I never would have foreseen that you would
begrudge my good fortune. I understand now,
that I am everything you are not.

 Circumstance has revealed you to be an
envious, it's true. You were not worthy of my
loyalty. I was too good a friend for you.
The lies that you tell don't hurt me anymore,
its simple old pal I am over you.

Drunken Shrew

Look at you my drunken shrew, intoxicated to the brim.

You swore to me, no more drink last night, Today your three sheets to the wind.

What am I to do, my drunken shrew?

As with you this demise is painful. You have stopped my heart, I am not sure it will restart, As this disease has made us unstable.

Enjoy

Enjoy each day as if it's your last.

That is what the elders say,

But if you don't know joy, real love or loss,
Each day remains the same.

Have Faith

Have faith my friend. This is not the end.
Your dream has stalled. So what?

Why can't it happen to you? You are human
too, pause is not failure, you require more
time on the clock.

Dream your dream and ensure that it's big,
Redeem all that the universe has apportioned
for you.

Do not mope or skulk, when life loosens the
rope. As all your dreams will not fall to dust,
They will rise up to you.

Believe in the divine, because it's bigger than
you. Discover the passion that god has given
to you.

Redeem all of your blessings pre written for
you. And succeed in the knowledge that faith
has delivered you.

Pray for breath to give life to your dreams,
Ask the Lord to give you the strength to
succeed.

Unswervingly hold up this vision to be true.
Then deliver your greatest accomplishment to
you.

Firefly

You are my firefly.

Bright and luminous, your light never dies.
You are always with me. My guiding light.
Ensuring that I get through my dark dark
nights.

You help me see the shade. Illuminating on the
people that hold me in contempt. Highlighting
all possibilities when my vision is skewed.
Forcing and pushing my tired spirit through.

Fore you are my firefly,

Consistent, robust, your light never
lies, I'm going to need you forever, So
don't you die?

Fore your light always sees me through.

Geraldine

Love me

Hate me

Berate me or

Manipulate me

For its cash money
money Cash money
money.

Kick me

Beat me

Rape me

Or simply
mistreat me. For
its cash money
money. Cash
money money.

This is my life. Some say a living hell. For me
its independence compared to many I am
doing well.

Hooker, whore, prostitute and more is how
society has labelled me. Where was this
society when my stepfather was raping me?

At twelve I ran from a life that was called home
I ran to the streets, where the remainder of my
innocence was thrown.

Thrown to my pimps, my punters, my drug
dealers. I then gave the rest of me to my
dealers. They promised security, peace and
serenity. They took the very heart of me,
until nothing was left in me.

A strong whore that's me for I am just 23. A
survivor I am, but that is not what I want to
be.

Circumstances have reduced me. So when
you see me don't you dare judge me. I am
you, but in me. I am knowledgeable in the
fact that I know my pimp, pimps me.

Not some sexual deviant
fantasy, It's just sex for sale,
baby.

Don't you dare judge me.

And you can keep your precious society.
Save your pity.

I am you in me,

We do it for the same
god, For it's for cash
money money Cash
money money.

Goodbye Beloved
For my sister carol RIP

When I heard the news you left this world. I
literally fell off my chair. The shock and grief
that engulfed me, I just was not prepared.

I raced with haste to the hospital. To view
your lifeless body lying there, with the tube
still intubated and your night dress on. I see
you too were caught unawares.

I could not comprehend you passing like this,
I began to wonder, What your last drink?
The last thing you said? The last laugh that
you had? And the last person that you
kissed.

Your death, although peaceful, was sudden,
therefore it felt violent in some way.

The one saving grace is that you felt nothing,
well that's what the autopsy states.

Your passing still haunts me as I often
wonder, did you know?

That the life you were expecting to wake up
to, slipped away in the night unbeknown.

Gratitude

Gratitude does not degrade you.

You are not demeaned by saying "Thank you."

Son that attitude does not help you. Fore you think that this is all yours.

Take the lessons I have given you.

Decline from professing the untruths.

Get off your soapbox, Address the real truth.

That is,

Your life. Your Future. Your naked truths.

I Miss you Mum

It's been a decade since you have been gone, I miss you more today, as I have so much more going on.

Without your counsel I have taken some missteps. Although, I am gutted that you are gone. Mum I do not have regrets.

Whilst you were with me I did what I needed to, I was a good daughter, I was always here for you.

I miss you so very much. Especially that laugh of yours. You were a naturally funny woman. You did not even have to try. When you recounted the stories of your life, you often made me cry.

What a special woman you were, to see the humor in everything.

Even the most painful things that people would say, you would find humor in it, and go about your day.

Now that temper of yours. Let's not go there.

You made confident men shy. I knew deep down they were scared. Your no nonsense attitude made you respected and feared.

Your kindness was legendary. Your heart truly big. There are so many things that defined you. It's those qualities I hold in high regards, and pray I have them deep within.

Now I am here alone without you. I simply have to say. I miss you mummy, each and every day, this void you left has not been filled. Well-meaning people often try. But the fact remains, you're gone and I am still in pain, and when I think of you I often cry.

Love you

X

In your Essence

Your power is in your essence.
So do not surrender it to love.

Don't fall in love. Stand up in
it. You can be strong yet sweet
like a Dove.

Our power is in our essence.
We should wield and shape
that tool.

Our essence is not just beauty. It's our
minds and spirits too.

It's the fundamentals that embody us. It's the
core of our goodness that swells.

Your power is in your essence. So, whatever
you do. Do not be afraid.
Your power is never wrong or
cruel, it's not vindictive, its full
of purpose not hate.

Never take it for granted. Allow your inner
substance to lead you through.

Your power is in your essence so allow your
essence to be the guide of you.

Like the last Time

This Pain is raw but as hurtful like before. The rain within just did not pour. My feelings were hurt, but I wasn't burnt to a crisp. Not like the last time.

The love that crippled me seems so far away. That pain and grief has not gone away. Every day is new and fresh for a start, but the experience of last time is here deep in my heart.

New loves come and go, old flames say cheerio, My heart is still searching, and my barriers keep rising, because of last time.

Will old age see me single? Will I have the courage to try and again and mingle? Will I ever have any children? Or will the last time keep me in my box. Crippled with fear and my heart the equinox. Will the sun shine on my heart again? Or did the sun set on last time.

Love to Emotions

Let your emotions run free with me.

Baby do not be afraid to experience the
feeling of total fulfilment with me.

Understand that you and I possess that
special chemistry. That transcends into the
divine energy that bonds two people forever.

Don't you understand that your mind has to
be free, to ensure that your heart can accept
me into you, and you into me?

My love do not be afraid. I have searched my
whole life to you. I am your inspiration and
you are mine too.

Understand me, Understand my needs,
Penetrate my soul, So when I am in pain You
feel my woes.

When you are weak, I will transcend my
strength through your veins I will be the one
to heal your pains.

I promise you that together our minds will be
free, and our bodies will experience pleasures
eternally.

And when that special day comes, your seeds
will be sown, and we shall nurture and
protect them until the life of our spirit has
gone.

Let your emotions run free with me, So
that we can enjoy the sweet ecstasy of
eternal love.

Love, Guilt and Shame

The first time I saw you with your swollen black eye, you looked in my face and blatantly lied, "I slept walked in the dark and I hit my head, I woke up this morning and my eye was so red".

The next time I saw you, your arm was in a cast, you knew how I would react, and before I could ask, "I fell down two steps, and put my arm out to protect my head" Tsk Tsk was all that I said.

After the arm break, our meetings were not frequent but few, I just wanted you to tell me, you didn't, so I tried to speak to you.

You got angry and slapped me, and screamed "You jealous cow, he loves me, find your own man and stop judging me."

I screamed "my love let me tell you, his fist tells no lies. He does not love you he hates you. He is going to keep blackening those eyes. Why should you suffer his violent attacks, better still get a knife and stab that bugger in his back. Report him to the police, press charges and put him away. If you don't want to do that for god's sake leave him today.

Come let me take you somewhere where you
are safe and not frightened to sleep. A place
you're not raped and beaten as part of his
routine.

Take my hand you deserve better than this.
You are my sister and I love you. Don't let
him get away with this."

The call that I have been waiting for, finally
came. You were in Acoma. There is no
activity in your brain.

The kicks to your head, broke both of your
jaws. The forearm that had healed was broken
once more. Your spleen he had ruptured as
he kicked you down the stairs.

Your skull cracked right open as he split it
with the chair. As I looked at you in the bed,
tubes coming out of here, and going into
there, I became weak. I had left you there!

How could I have left you with that monster
knowing your pain?

This man who was your tormentor time and
time again. What kind of sister am I? I left
you for dead. This day was expected, I
already played it in my head.

The reality set in, and I could not breathe. Am
I co-conspirator to your murder, as I did
nothing to make him leave?

The rest is a blur as the rage had set in. My sister was a domestic abuse victim. I just sat and waited here. I saw him staggering up the road.

My heart was racing and my rage was pacing as I knew I would not let this go.

As he crossed the road, I turned the keys to start her up. I revved up my truck, and I wished the bastard good luck.

I smashed into his body with full velocity of my truck, and continued driving to the hospital, where I sat and held my sisters hand.

I looked at her lovingly and whispered in her ear. "He too is gone now my dear. You can leave in peace knowing he will not do this again. I did it. I got him. Have peace and go to Grandpa Vin."

Me, I am in prison serving a short jail time. I had a good lawyer and I think lady luck was on my side.

The jury was with me, we showed them what he did. It doesn't excuse my actions, but they could see he was a pig.

I am sorry for what I did, truly I am. He is gone forever, but so is my sister Sam.

My Beautiful Black Man

Potential is not a word used to describe you.
You are despised by many and only respected
by few.

Never mind all the educated, hardworking,
stable fathers that we have.

The media focuses on the negative. They are
never objective, and can be oh so selective,
with the stories they can tell.

My beautiful, delectable, strong, iridescent
black man.

Whom is my king, and I am his Queen as
only you know how to treat me like the black
pearl that I am.

Stand Tall.

Hold your head high.

Command Respect!

You have come from a people who have
struggled from day one.

From Tribesmen, who have fought wars and
won.

Throughout our history you have been belittled and denied.

Take your throne in life and never be side-lined

My Son

Your breath was soft and smelt sweet like
honey dew.

Baby skin so fresh, it glistening.
Your cry so new, the sound of you
was so exhilarating.

My drugged up state, did not sedate the
feelings of motherhood.

It was a classical moment,
intoxicatingly flawless, I cannot
believe it's so good. My stance of
perfection was previously
misunderstood.

You are perfection personified, and this is
motherhood.

You are impeccable, untarnished and
untouched.

My son I have waited so long for you.
With so many false starts I never thought
this would be possible.

I am here, your mother and am so humbled
at your touch.

This is our time.

As I long as I have life in my
lungs, my son you will always be
mine.

NEO

For Samantha and David

To the parents of this baby thank you for Neo
your blessed child

For his cheeky spirit, those perfect dimples
and his beautiful brown eyes

This child come from pure love

Not just from a superficial fling

But a love that derives from god, which
means this love is everlasting.

God love in unconditional, unequivocal,
passionate and true

The way that gods loves all things, is the
same way you love Neo too.

Tough love, is God's love which we will
never forget But this love,

Our Love will ensure this boy will become a
great man yet.

No Stones

History supplies us with stories of strength,
irrespective the culture or the continent.
Our brilliance and genius circulates the
globe. We are separate, yet united, in this
sublunary world.

Audacious, indomitable, valiant examples of
us all around,

We are aunties, sisters, grandmothers,
daughters, mothers and friends, continually
striving, developing and achieving to the end.

We are stronger than they gives us credit for.

More brilliant than they can see.

Our right is to continue to sing our praises,
We must provide ovation for women like you
and me.

Our movement has moved forward. We are a long way from the end. Women are sold as chattel in 2016, when will slavery end.

Young girls stolen because they choose to be educated; FGM is still rife; Unequal pay is not a thing of the past; We are still fighting the corporate world fight. We are bombarded with images that are demeaning, many of them are just not true.

Come on sisters let's take charge. There is still a lot to do. Get involved, support one another, and join a charity if you can.

If you can't there is no judgement here for you. Remember this, like a lingering kiss, no matter what we think.

Those stones represent requiescence, and for most men life is bliss.

Phony

That phony personality is quite frankly your reality. You are a "stinking peacock" for all to see.

 You ruffle your feathers. And stretch them out for display. And shout to the world, " Look at me!"
You are a lip server. You want to be "me", you imposter. Yet you always manage to say the right things.

But when my back is turned, the masquerade returns. Back slider friend, that is when you push the sharp knife in.

Reality

Talentless, classless reality stars making money Putting out their "everything" for all to see.

Calling this real life and their reality. We observe their lives like bees, gravitating to their fodder like honey.

Tell Lie Vision is what we believe.

Tell Lie Vision is what we perceive to be true, Deep down we know that this reality is fabricated for me and you.

What is it that we are missing?

What is it that we crave?

When we run home to watch the Kardashians just living and embellishing their day to day.

What are we missing?

What is it that we crave?

When Tell Lie Vision, rather than books is what we rely on to educate.

E News is addictive but it's full of nonsense and crap. This voyeuristic addiction is a luring honey trap.

Most kids today are hooked on this desire for fame. Fame for the game, fame with no shame. Fame for their asses, their lips and brash tactics. Fame for hip hop wives that clashes. Fame for the C listers that sit in that house, filled with broken souls who are looking for a route out.

We, You and I are to blame.

I admit it. I watch trash TV and I feel no shame. But after a while when the trash sinks in, I wonder what I could have been doing. I understand the conspiracy with the Tell Lie Team.

It's to brainwash people like you and me. We buy into happiness that stems from material things.

We envy the diamonds and the sparkly rings, Their bank accounts are visible, money is overflowing from their well.

Make up flawless, lights on, cameras rolling, and its show and tell.

What is the price of this instantaneous fame? When the camera goes off, what is left is it shame?

The price that is paid, is no privacy at all. Fame for fames sake has insurmountable flaws. There are hordes of spectators who have opinions about you. The press who are waiting to lambaste you. Random spectators whose tongues are like swords, has opinion about everything that belong to you and yours. The laceration from the humiliation when your spouse steps out of line.

The very fact that you have to read about their infidelity in the national enquirer online. The price that you pay for no privacy at all, makes my quest for success dwindle and fall. I will move on and so will you. We are fickle you see and the rest of them too.

Within our day to day we will be sold something new.

This ode is not to hate but to relate to you an observation.

P.D. LORDE

Life is for living and not this voyeuristic
obsession. Do not believe what you are fed
through this tell lie vision maze.

Prepare for a life filled with love and ambition.
Do not concern yourself with what others
have, as that is not happiness, it's the Tell
Live Vision trap.

Superpatriot

Who do you think you are? Talking to me like
that.

Do you feel superior, powerful, in control,
because you're not?

You are nothing more than an intolerable
super patriot.

The windows of your soul betray
you, I read the contempt in your
eyes.

Your body languages illustrates your venom,
bubbling up like a volcano, hot lather ready
to rise.

Your opinion is beneath me

I care not for your lack of self,

I was delivered by an Empress, Queen of
Queens, I am royalty and exude inner
wealth. Your tone of voice exposes you, it
does not matter to me.

Fore I am confident and prideful in who I am,
and all of my abilities.

My confidence offends you.
My brilliance blinds your eyes.

Every stab of I receive from your hateful
words, will never dim my light.

You wear your insecurities like a dirty old
shirt, Which fits you snugly by the way.

Your words were spoken to cause me harm,

I see that clearly now. The pride and strength
within my veins rehabilitates and dries my
eyes.

It angers you to see that I am unperturbed by
you.

You're affronted by my nerves of steel, what
more can this bigot do.

I am regal, omnipresent, stupendous and
profound.

Deep down you know this to be true.

Your bigoted ways will rear its head again
and I will be waiting for you.

TOLERATE

T-O-L-E-R-A-T-E

This is what you expect of me?

My colour

My creed

My sex

My race

My gender

My religion

My politics

My faith

TOLERATE

What more is required for *you* to see *me!*

I'm rich

I'm poor

I'm black

I'm white

I'm Jewish

I'm Muslim

Are these any reasons to fight?

We kill for money. Being poor is seen as a sin. Skin colour is a weapon, and can make you a victim.

Religion starts wars. Or do they? Or is that *just* Man. Why should I die a martyr forsaking all that I am? Tell me who am I, and what do you see?

 A religion, A colour, A gender,
Or just me!

We are one you and I. We are a part of the human family We belong to **MAN – Kind**.

We all share a family tree.

Superficiality divides us,

Hatred ignites us,

The media manipulates us, So don't just tolerate me, Accept me.

True Love

I was young and impressionable,

However, I loved you for sure. It was deeper
than any valley.

My love was purer than pure.

You made me a woman, And enabled me to
feel. When you told me that you loved me, It
was forever. My dreams became real.

You said that you loved me. I was the only
woman for you. I even met your parents and
loved them through and through.

This pretense you kept going for as long as
you could. You loved me, I know this. Yet
had a unruly manhood.

My heart broken. My emotions all in tatters.
My head swirled with your words of love.
Your lies had me shattered.

Years on I reflect and wonder how you are.
You will always be my one true love. I have
lived my life loving through your scars.

War

Man loves war and war loves man.

We've been destroying one another since time
has begun.

The tragedies that surround us have been
here before.

That feeling of hopelessness engulfs mankind
once more.

We cannot surrender to the fears within,

Yet, we hang on the propaganda spoken by

these powerful men.

Man loves war and war loves man.

We've been destroying one another since time
has begun.

The motives are similar, the rhetoric is the
same. The fight is for land, freedom, and oil.

There are too many excuses to proclaim.

Who is the victim or victor at war.

The powerful that start them are shielded,
Unlike the weak and the poor.

Who is the victor?

Who ultimately gains?

The manufacturers of machine guns, missiles

and death planes,

Man loves war and war loves man.

We've been destroying one another since time
has begun,

What a price?

What a life?

What is the price for a life these days?

Bodies blown open by war.

Government   handouts   renders
wounded soldiers penniless and poor.

What a price for a life of principle, What a
price for a life of courage, What a price for a
life of vigor.

These young soldiers they seemed so
invincible.

Man loves war and war loves man.

Politician and dictators have been destroying
human beings since time began.

What If?
Inspired by Lisa Nicholls

What if?

I got out of my way and pursued my dreams.

I believed in myself.

I set my greatness free.

What if?

I listened to my inner voice.

My champion within.

My ultimate force.

What if?

I just accepted myself.

My good bits and sad bits,

Loving me through sickness and health.

What if?

I just loved me for me.

Without persecuting and obliterating my
inner personality.

What if?

I adore the cellulite on my thighs.

And embraced my soft tummy,
And the fat pods above my
eyes.

What if?

I made mediocracy a thing of the past.

Lived my life in my brilliance

Stood in my light.

And projected my dynamite.

What if?

I only thought positive things,

And sat with likeminded people,

Filled with possibility

And tremendous gifts.

What if?

I allowed myself to dream BIG!

Take this journey on faith.

And changed my universe from within.

What if?

I realised that the power of my mind,

Could shape realities,

Dictate my dreams,

Exceed all my expectations and Create my
New Fabulous Life!

What if?

What if?

What if?

ROOTS

ROOTS. I am not talking about the colour of my hair, or the legs that germinate from seeds embedded deep in the soil beneath me.

ROOTS. You may have the knowledge of where you belong, the tribe, people and country of where you come from. It is sad for me to say that I cannot be judicious regarding my family tree, to put it bluntly, I have a limited history. Two generations, maybe three tops, this is where on paper my lineage stops.

ROOTS. I have found that it so important to belong, which means going backwards to proceed forwards is how to move on. It's like the foundations of a house, without it the building is not strong. There is nothing untoward about wanting to know the actual country, not continent that I originate from.

ROOTS. 60 Million Africans died in the crossing. The people that survived the floating pit of damnation lived a life without dignity and were steeped in degradation.

ROOTS: 60 Million, that is a ratio 1 in 3 people being murdered each day in every country until the next century. Yet, there was no outcry or even any shame. I am living proof that many survived as I am a proud descendant of a slave.

ROOTS. Many critics say that it's time to move on and deal with today. To a degree I can see that contention. When I pause, and reflect some more, I sense that the critiques have a deeper connection to their own blood line and reflection.

ROOTS. My pride is strong with my connection to Jamaica. I am British, that's it. I am bloody proud of it. I recognise good old Regina's contribution. From implementing the slave trade to being the leaders of change. I acknowledge the benefaction that this country made. Fore we put the world to shame. Lord Wilberforce lead way to eradicate that despicable trade.

ROOTS. My Children will learn of the history that we have been given. I hope and pray that tolerance and understanding will reign free. I fear for their future as I see the legacy of Jim Crowism living and spreading their poison to many.

ROOTS. It is powerful to know that your roots and my roots will come together in one common place. That is humanity. Our heart does not care of skin colour, creed, sexual orientation, religion or disability. All life is sacred and equal so all people must be able to live free. We should all be free from persecution and war. The world must be set free from cowboy politicians that beat down the poor, who alienate allies to bring only war to our doors. We should be free to love whomever we choose. Women must be free to decide on which body parts we want to use. We should live free from hate, rape and abduction. Free to educate and liberate third world mothers who have nothing.

ROOTS. We will come together as one. Fore no matter what our history is all our roots belong.

ABOUT THE AUTHOR

P.D LORDE is mother to three beautiful boys and live in the East of England with her husband and children. She has been writing poetry since the age of eight years old and short stories and novels since the aged of eleven. As a young child she has been surrounded by energetic and passionate storytellers within her family. Her early influences were Dr Maya Angerlou, Beatrix Potter, Terry McMillian, Barbara Taylor Bradford, Steven King to name a few. After graduating with honors degree in Law in the late 90's she pursued a career within the legal field. Only since her forties has she gained the confidence to share with the world a collection of her work

88546670R00043